DRUNKS OF THE FRENCH QUARTER THEATRE

DRUNKS OF THE FRENCH QUARTER THEATRE

ELAINE ALLEN

Special thanks to all my first readers: Jazmine Carroll, Emilie Allen, Iris Dauterman, and Richard Sprenkle.

Also, thanks to all the people who followed my posts online and told me this could be a book.

Thanks to my mother for tolerating my constant stress about writing, and to Richard for dealing with late night panics about formatting and helping me make my Fleur De Lis look like something an adult made.

Last, but not least, thank you for reading.

CONTENTS

Introduction

Welcome to the French Quarter, one of the most historic neighborhoods in New Orleans! Whether you are visiting our neighborhood, live here, or just dream of wandering our streets, I hope this book can give you at least an inkling of what it feels like to be in the heart of the Big Easy. I am a tour guide in the French Quarter, spending my evenings shouting history at drunk tourists on the side of the road, and so I get to hear and see many of New Orleans' best and worst locals, transplants, and visitors. The French Quarter is often a hot mess, but it is a fun one, so please enjoy these messy moments.

I have tidied up some exceptionally confusing phrasing, added context when I felt it was needed, and changed names in the rare occasions that I heard them so that no one can be identified, but I want you to know that everything in this book is something I have heard or seen in public in New Orleans. I have also included a glossary of pertinent New Orleans-specific terms in the back of the book to help make sense of those things that might be clearer if you knew local nomenclature. I will warn you there will be inappropriate comments, naughty words, and horrifying actions. There will not be much logic.

So welcome, enjoy the chaos, but know that if you come here and say something ridiculous, there may be someone listening.

Laissez Les Bon Temps Rouler

(Let the Good Times Roll)

(2:30 A.M. We are far enough from Bourbon street for the world to be quiet and dark. An obviously drunk man walks down the sidewalk mumbling just loudly enough that it's not clear if he is talking to someone else or himself.)

Man: Late. I got to get there, and I got to get drunk. I'm late. I'm supposed to be singing on Decatur right now. I'm late, and I got to get there and sing for my supper. Or my drinks. Supposed to be singing for three hours. Gonna sing my heart out.

(He walks by a young woman who is unlocking her car. He does not stop, but he turns to watch her as he walks.)

Man: And I'm gonna be singing about you. *(Pointing at young woman)* Because I am head over heels in love with you right now.

Young Woman: Thank you?

Man: Alright, now. Just know I'm singing about you. Drive safe, now.

(He nods, smiling, and she does the same. They go their separate ways.)

(A well-dressed girl is sitting with the gutter-punks along Decatur. They are sharing a cigarette while she tells them a long-winded story.)

Gutter-punk: And who was Chelsea?

Yuppie: She's my best friend. The first girl I ever broke into a house with!

(A woman leans against a lamp post, illuminated by a circle of warm light on an otherwise dark corner of Esplanade. She is reading a book. All is quiet, until a couple stumble down from the heart of the Quarter, the woman barely upright, supported by the man.)

Woman 2: *(Pointing at the reader.)* See that? I would love to do that! Why can't I just read a book on the street?

(They stumble by, the woman still watching the reader. They are across the street when she suddenly shouts.)

Woman 2: What are you reading???

(A drunk couple walk down the street. Every item they pass on the sidewalk – balcony posts, trash cans, window frames – the woman points at.)

Woman: *(Monotone)* Hit that! Hit that! Hit that!

(The man stumbles along behind, staring at every item she points at, but never touching any of them.

Woman: *(Stopping and turning to look at him)* See! I care. I tell you what we are passing, and you hit it.

(The man does not respond. Not noticing she has stopped, he stumbles into her.)

(Two people are walking down Royal Street. The man walks a few feet in front of the woman. They walk smoothly, without any stumbles or signs of difficulty. The woman is not even wobbling on her heels.)

Woman: *(To the guy)* Man. You are just so good at walking...

(He does not respond, nor look at her. It is not entirely clear if he is aware she is behind him.)

(A cop car blocks an intersection a block away from the chaos of Bourbon Street. Next to it, two gentlemen are having a discussion. This discussion seems to involve a lot of laughter, broad gestures, and slurring. One of them attempts to casually lean on a stop sign, misses, and bangs his face into the sign.)

Guy 1: Shit! That hurt.

Guy 2: Sssssssshush. Not so loud. *(Pointing at the bemused police officers)* They'll notice you're drunk.

(A suburban, middle-class, middle-aged couple walk down Decatur Street, watching the city pass by them. A bike krewe pass: dozens of young people riding bikes with neon lights on the spokes and speakers blasting music. Some of the bikes are personalized, low-rider bikes and tricycles, with individual paint jobs. The riders are screaming along to the lyrics of the music blasting from the speakers, interspersed with random "Whoooooooooo"ing when the lyrics are too far beyond them.)

Suburban Woman: *(To her man)* Do you think they've been drinking?

Suburban Man: Maybe...

Suburban Woman: Should we call someone?

(A couple walk down the street, arm in arm, though it's not clear whether that's for romance or stability.)

Man: I'm not so drunk that I can't say knee bra... *(Tries again)* In knee bro... *(Tries again)* In-Eee-Breei-Ated. Inebriated. I'm not so drunk I can't say drunk.

Woman: Exactly.

(A grocery store in the heart of the Quarter. A man wearing a hat with the word "cocaine" printed in the letters you buy to put your address on your mailbox is having a shouted conversation with one of the cashiers as he heads out the door.)

Cocaine Dude: You have a good weekend, now!

Cashier: Your Fireball is sticking out of your pocket.

Cocaine Dude: Cool. *(Taking the bottle to have a swig)* Man, I've been doing this a long time. I party hard Thursday through Monday, go to jail Tuesday and Wednesday, and I'm out in time for Thursday. Man, I'm 45. I have been doing this a long time.

Cashier: Haven't we all? You have a good weekend, too!

(Five men all wearing beads and backwards-facing baseball caps are gathered on Royal Street. They shout. They cheer. One humps a stop sign. A nearby local pulls out their phone to call the cops. One of our drunk heroes dashes across the street to an open door.)

Guy 1: Dude! Over here!

(He points inside. It is an art gallery. The guys stare in at the three-foot-tall concrete lawn statues on display.)

Guy 1: Let's go in here!

Guy 2: Yeah! Let's go steal some STATUES!!!!!

(They cheer and storm into the store, while the sales associate rushes forward to stop them.)

(Two women stand on the sidewalk outside a nice restaurant: the kind of place where people still dress for dinner. They are looking down with slightly exasperated looks on their faces. Their friend is laying on her back on the sidewalk, sweating and rubbing her forehead. Tears are streaming from her eyes. She is gasping. A woman walks by, stops, and walks back to check on them.)

Passerby: Are y'all alright?

Woman: Yeah. She's fine.

Passerby: Did she get too hot? Do y'all need some water?

Woman: Nope. She ate a pepper.

(Two women loaded down with huge bags of souvenirs walk by the giant text on the awning at Cafe du Monde that says it's open 24 hours.)

Woman 1: *(With a thick midwestern accent)* Oh my God! Sheila! This place is open 24 hours!

Woman 2: A Day?!

(Jackson Square, near dusk. The Cathedral looms elegantly over artists selling their wares and buskers playing everything from Indian Harp to Pickle Tub Drums. Tourists in shirts that read "I Got Bourbon Faced on Shit Street" or "Drunk 1" are everywhere. A little boy of perhaps nine-years-old runs around in circles between the poles that keep cars from driving into the square.)

Boy: SUGAR! Sugar! SUGAR! SUGAR! Sugar! Sugar! SUGAR! Sugar! Sugar! Sugar! SUGAR!

(A few feet away a woman sits with her head in her hands. She has a sunburn, stains down her shirt, and a stroller with a sleeping baby in front of her.)

Woman: Yeah. We're having beer for dinner.

(Two older locals are standing in front of one of the last bars before Bourbon turns into a quiet residential street. They are holding beers and ignoring a car trying to inch by them.)

Guy 1: I think I'm still drunk from the Chewbacchus Parade, and next week is Krewe Du Vieux, so my apartment has no furniture. It's just beads. Like just stacks of beads in the shape of chairs.

Guy 2: It's fine. You can stay with me.

(A tour is gathered just off Bourbon Street. The guide shouts full volume to be heard over the pounding rhythm of dance music from the bars. As the guide starts talking about an old convent, a pair walk off of Bourbon towards the group.)

Man: Hey! A ghost tour! Look! A ghost tour!

(The guide ignores him.)

Man: *(Louder)* Yeah! Ghost Tour! Do you know where we can get some weed?

(The guide ignores him. He walks up right behind her.)

Man: *(Yelling right in her ear)* Hey! Ghost group! Where can I get some weed?

(Giving up, she spins to address him.)

Tour Guide: We are in the middle of a story, so if you could move along...

Man: *(Still shouting)* But do you know where me and my son can get some weed?

Tour Guide: No. I don't.

(The man shrugs and leads his maybe twelve-year-old son away from the horrified tour, back towards Bourbon Street.)

(It's a Monday, but Bourbon Street still glows with light and thrums with sound – music and drunken shouting. Less than a block away, the decadence has faded, the streets fading to quiet and twilight. An occasional noxious smell is the only sign of how close we are to the cluster of bars and clubs. Two middle-aged, well-put-together, blonde women walk towards the calm.)

Woman 1: *(Sounding disappointed)* I expected girls flashing their boobs for beads and shots.

Woman 2: *(Equally disappointed)* It's nothing like I've seen on TV.

12

Confused Screaming

(A woman stands on a corner of Bourbon Street. She leans against a pole supporting a gallery and stares at her phone as drunk people stream by, lights flash, and music pounds through the 19th century buildings. A guy walks up to her.)

Guy: *(Louder than necessary.)* Ma'am! There's a unicorn on your shoulder.

(She ignores him.)

Guy: No, really. I'm not hitting on you. There's a unicorn.

(She turns to find one of the mule buggies has stopped while trying to cross the street. The mule is white, with glittery-gold painted hooves, wings on her harness, and a plastic horn on her bridle. The mule's face is hovering right over the woman's shoulder.)

Woman: *(Clearly startled.)* Oh! Hello.

Buggy Driver: *(To mule)* Come on, Claudia! Give the lady personal space.

(A belligerent frat guy wanders down the quiet end of Bourbon Street, well past the point where the bars peter out and the area transitions back into a quiet residential neighborhood.)

Belligerent Frat Guy: *(Shouting at the houses.)* WAKE UP! WAKE UP! WAKE UP!

(A middle-aged guy is sitting on his porch, watching. As the frat guy nears, he laughs.)

Middle-aged Guy: *(With an Irish Channel Accent)* She always said she would rather be tickled to death than stabbed. That's why when she asks for six inches, you give it to her twice.

(Frat Guy pauses. He looks confused. He continues down the street, silently.)

(Late summer evening. The world is just beginning to cool down enough to live a normal life. A man stands outside of a bar, dressed as a sexy Santa. He is wearing red, fuzzy short-shorts, trimmed with fake white fur, with a fuzzy red jacket, also trimmed in white, hanging open over his waxed naked chest. He is smoking with a friend.)

Friend: I was raised in this ultra-Christian church...

Sexy Santa: Man. I was raised by a see-saw!

(He pauses, clearly waiting for laughter. His friend just looks confused.)

(A party of casually dressed, mild-aged folks walk down Royal Street, past dozens of art galleries. The bright afternoon sun highlights their khaki pants and pastel shirts. They look like they wandered out of ad for a yacht club.)

Man: She can't be your arch nemesis. You were the officiant at her wedding...

(A woman dressed in the cliché, sexy witch costume – a leotard, tutu, and witch's hat – talks to a man in a unicorn onesie in the middle of an intersection. It is Halloween night.)

Girl: Mmmmm?

Guy: Mmmmm...

Girl: MMMmmmmmmmmMMM??

Guy: Hmmmmm!? *(Pause.)* What? No.

(A Woman in a corset and not much else coming running down the street towards them.)

New Girl: My People! You. My People!

Girl: MMMMMMMmmmmmmmmm!

New Girl: What?

Girl: Yes! We are your people!

New Girl: The rest of the group's up here.

Girl: We thought we left you behind.

Guy: *(Quietly, as if to himself)* Mmmmmmmm.

(A woman walks by with a girl who looks to be her adult daughter. They are weighed down with dozens of shopping bags from souvenir shops.)

Mom: ...and I'll get the laser grits to burn away all the junk in my trunk.

Daughter: I'm still skeptical about this operation. Are you sure that's what the doctor said?

(They pass by. I, too, am skeptical about this operation.)

(Two girls stand in front of an art gallery which for some reason has a life-sized cardboard cut-out of Queen Elizabeth II in the window. They take a picture standing next to the cut-out, examine the photo, and then try again.)

Girl 1: I wish I was the Queen of Switzerland.

Girl 2: Now, don't be mean. She's not here to defend herself.

Girl 1: What?

(Vibrant brass and syncopated rhythms fill the air. We are outside of a bar on the edge of Frenchmen Street. Inside the bar, people are dancing. Outside, people bob along to the music while they smoke cigarettes. A group of very drunk men in polo shirts and cargo shorts walk out of the bar where the jazz band plays.)

Guy 1: Aww Man! That's some of that fifties shit. That tuba and shit! Why are they playing fifties shit? Who wants to hear that shit? *(He pauses, then laughs.)* Wait. It's not a tuba. It's the other one.

Guy 2: Trumpet?

Guy 1: Yeah, Trumpet. *(He mimes playing the trombone.)*

Guy 3: Yeah. You were a trumpet guy, right?

Guy 1: Yeah, man. I played it in high school.

(Reader, it was a trombone.)

(Pirate's Alley Café. A bar smaller than most people's living room, with bare minimum lighting, dark wood walls, and a big wooden bar that takes up the majority of the floorspace. A man dressed as a pirate stands in the middle of the space, alone except for the bartender and a pair of tourists, half-in and half-out of the door. The tourists are clearly rethinking their patronage of this bar.)

Pirate: *(Singing)* Mexican Americans just like to be Mexican Americans...

(The tourists leave.)

(Three drunk women stumble out of a dark, empty bar. One of the women grabs her friends by the arms, pulling them swiftly aside from the doorway.)

Woman: Step to the left! Make room. There are like 900 assholes behind us.

(The bartender looks around the empty bar, obvious confusion on his face. There is no one behind them.)

(An old food truck is sitting on the side of Decatur Street. Its window is open, showing a little room occupied by a piano, a beaded curtain, and several tapestries. A woman sits at the piano while a man stands on the street in front of the truck with a harmonica. Together, they play "The Battle Hymn of the Republic" to an audience of gutter-punks and their dogs. A group of loud, drunk girls walk by, one humming along.)

Girl: I recognize this song.

Humming Girl: Yeah.

Girl: I think I remember it from vacation bible school.

Humming Girl: Nope. It's Ed Sheeran.

(Two women walk down the street. One is decked out in several layers of ripped shirts, fishnet stockings, and faded black denim. The other wears a brown plaid shirt and oversized glasses. Both are walking in the street, even though the sidewalk is empty and cars are coming up behind them. Both are carrying beers in oversized cans. A car honks at them.)

Girl 1: You know, they just passed a law. There's now a seven-day waiting period before you can buy a doorknob!

(A man stands in Jackson Square, screaming hate, obscenities, and anger into the ether. He is calling everyone in earshot every cuss word in the book. Tourists look on nervously, giving him a wide berth. One of the men who hangs out in the square on a regular basis stands up.)

Regular: Look. If you're going to make a fool of yourself like this in public, you need to take yourself elsewhere.

(The screamer persists, turning his anger on the regular, using a whole lot of X-rated language that basically amounts to "you can't make me" before finally shouting...)

Screamer: F-you! You need to respect your elders!

Regular: Suck my nuts! My mother's your age, and she'll come out here and kick your ass!

(Two groups of mustachioed men pass each other on the street, one carrying glasses of wine, the other all in red makeshift dresses. The Wine Guys raise a glass to the Red Dresses, while each group has separate conversations.)

Wine Guy: Yeah, and by the fourth one, I was calling it pané and garnishing it with a hundred-dollar bill....

Red Dress 1: *(Talking to his friends)* We'll just tell them we're from Vermont and have a startup maple syrup conglomerate.

Red Dress 2: I don't know if they'll buy it...

Wine Guy: *(Suddenly looking back at Red Dresses)* I don't know what you're talking about, but I'd invest!

(Three twenty-somethings stand outside the Cornstalk Fence Hotel, all holding jewel-bright mixed drinks.)

Guy: But you can't renovate this place, because it's on the Universal Department of Interior Registry.

Girl 1: Oh, damn! That's crazy

Girl 2: Do you mean States United Department of the Interior Registry?

Guy: Yeah, the United States Historical State Registry Department.

(A guy is walking his dog through Jackson Square. The dog is sniffing along, peacefully. The man seems a bit unfocused. The bells of St. Louis Cathedral ring the quarter hour.)

Guy: *(Flailing about as if he is boxing the sound.)* I'M ALLERGIC TO BELLS!

(The dog looks up at him with a clear "what the hell" expression on his puppy face. After a moment, the dog walks on. When the leash pulls him, the human follows.)

(Two girls are sitting on the front stairs of someone's house. They have both taken off their shoes and are holding their strappy heels in their hands. They lean against each other and stare out towards the skyline.)

Girl 1: If I die before you, you have to bury me below you.

Girl 2: *(Nodding)* Of course.

(A couple walk down a quiet street near the old Ursuline Convent. They are fighting, loudly.)

Woman: You made me go there, and no one likes me there, and IT STINKS!

Man: Well, I don't like you there either!

(They turn a corner. The sound of their voices echoing off the building obscures the woman's answer, but amplifies the sound, so we hear muffled anger for a sentence or two before quiet returns to the street. A few moments pass before they come back, their voices proceeding them by about half a block.)

Woman: I can't believe you made me go there!

Man: It was for ten minutes!

Woman: WE WERE SUPPOSED TO GO HOME AND FUCK, SHAWN! WE WERE SUPPOSED TO GO HOME AND FUCK!

Guy: I just wanted to get one drink.

Women: We were supposed to go home and fuck! We were supposed to have a romantic night.

Random Passerby: Chill out, guys. Where do you think we are? The Quarter?

(A group of twenty-somethings walk down Royal Street, past dozens of middle-class families and older retirees. One girl is walking like the guy from the ministry of silly walks: putting each leg about three feet in the air with each step.)

Girl: Don't mind me! I'm totally human!

(She spots someone sitting on a balcony above, watching her.)

Girl: Hello, up there! I swear I'm human!

(A woman is standing on the corner of Royal Street, ignoring the streams of people trying to get by her on one of the busiest streets in the Quarter. She has clearly been waiting for someone for a while and has lost what patience she ever had. She is now on her phone, one hand on her hip, tapping out an angry rhythm as she listens to whoever is on the other side of the line.)

Woman: Girl, I've been out here holding your hand and your hair back for two hours, and now you suddenly want to sober up?

(Pause)

Woman: You wanna be the drunk queen, but you ain't.

24

TMI

(It is Southern Decadence. A group of Christian missionaries stand on a little stage in the middle of Bourbon Street between two gay bars, with a contingent of cops keeping them separated from the revelry around them. The preacher's voice is amplified by speakers held on high by two aggressively blank-looking men in polo shirts. He has clearly been sermonizing for a while. Around him a crowd of men in harnesses, neon day-glow G-strings, mesh body suits, and leather puppy masks drink, dance, and watch him.)

Preacher: And Are You Willing to Condemn Your Soul to HELL for Turning your Back on God?!

(The crowd cheers.)

Preacher: How Will You Feel When Your Eternal Soul Burns in Hell, Tortured by Demons for Eternity!?

(The crowd cheers.)

Preacher: Whipped and Beaten Day and Night!

Voice From the Crowd: Oh YES, Daddy!

(More cheering.)

(A 40-ish man walks down the street with a woman of roughly the same age.)

Man: I don't mean to be gauche, but a friend of mine is dating this little orphan girl...

(Two women walk by the shops along Jackson Square. The sun shines through the oak trees in the park, the light dappling the flagstones.)

Woman 1: He and the dog have this bondage thing going on.

Woman 2: Did you mean bonding?

Woman 1: Yeah. Whatever.

(Two men stand outside of a gay bar. A group of wide-eyed tourists walk by, watching everything like a parade might pop out of a doorway at any moment.)

Guy 1: Oh my God! I need to go home and take care of my pussy!

Guy 2: Really? Do you need help?

Guy 1: Nope. My pussy isn't even big enough to ever touch the ground...

(The tourists walk on, more quickly than before, staring desperately ahead. The two guys snicker.)

(Four young men are walking a poodle down the surprisingly dark streets out past Lafitte's in Exile.)

Guy 1: I don't know what he said. I missed it. I was getting a blow job.

Guy 2: Must have been a good blow job.

Guy 1: Not really, but you know...

Guy 3: Yeah. It's just polite to pay attention.

(There are several groups of tourists sitting on the steps that lead down to the river across from Jackson Square. A family is taking pictures of the passing steamboat. A dog walker jogs by with two dogs on a leash. Two gutter-punks walk up from the train tracks.)

Gutter-punk 1: See, Satanists love me. We always get along, but I'm just not into that...

(Gutter-punk 2 points at a girl sitting on one of the benches.)

Gutter-punk 2: That's the kind of girl you like, right? She's got a good look. You'd hit that?

Gutter-punk 1: Yeah, I mean, sure. But now, Satanists...

(All is calm. A calm woman walks down the calm stretch of Royal Street past dozens of art galleries with her calm friend. It is quiet enough that we can hear even their muted conversation.)

Woman 1: *(Calmly)* She really does think her apartment is haunted.

Woman 2: *(Rolling her eyes)* Yeah, and I'm sure people died there, too.

(Three respectable looking adults stand near a mild neighborhood bar. Think more Cheers and less Coyote Ugly.)

Woman 1: *(While bouncing up and down)* Fuck Humanity! Fuck Humanity! Fuck Humanity!

(Her two companions shift away uncomfortably. The other people on the street look across at them curiously.)

Woman 2: Uhmm, alright...

Woman 1: No. You don't understand. It's okay. I'm a professor at *(REDACTED)* University.

(Three guys walk away from Clover Grill, two arm-in-arm, hands in each other's pockets. The third is a few feet behind, an obvious third wheel.)

Guy 1: *(To his partner)* Dude, sometimes I wish you weren't so nice to me.

Guy 3: Dude. He just called you a "fucking whore."

Guy 1: Yeah. And?

(Two tours pass each other like ships in the night, one going one way, one going the other. It is the kind of hot, muggy night where the air sits heavy on the lungs, and everyone's skin is perpetually clammy.)

One of the Tours: *(Cheering)* Go lightning! Whoo!

Guy from the Other Tour: Sure? Go lightning!

(Tour One high fives the other as they pass. At the end of the line is a little old lady with a walker and a sharp glare.)

Little Old Lady: I'm sweating my balls off here.

(A guy walks down a quiet back street having an exceptionally loud conversation on speakerphone.)
Guy: No. This is the first time in 24 hours I'm wearing clothes.

(We are on the steps leading down to the river. The water laps quietly against the bottom step, dark and light flashing in the moonlight. A couple of tourists admire the river. A busker rests after a long, humid day. A cook, still in uniform, enjoys a cigarette before heading home. An older man with a scraggly beard and dirty clothes sits on the steps leading down to the river. It is quiet except for the older man.)

Older Man: *(Shouting)* I could really use a cigarette.

(No one responds.)

Older Man: Hey! Y'all! Who's gonna give me a cigarette!

(No one responds.)

Older Man: I know one of you has to have a cigarette!

(A new guy arrives, walking down the steps to sit with his friend, and thus attracting the old man's attention.*)

Older Man: Hey. You! I've got two bucks I'll give you for a cigarette!

(No reply.)

Older Man: Hey! Don't ignore me! I need a cigarette.

(A couple of people shake their heads, muttering that they don't have any.)

Older Man: You don't got to be scared. I ain't dangerous. I ain't trouble. I've got top CIA clearance...

*Drunks, like the T-Rex in a certain movie, have vision-based movement.

(A couple stand on the platform with the cannon and benches between the river and Jackson Square. They stand arm-in-arm, quietly watching the mule buggies and tourists go by below. It is very romantic. Two men walk up the steps and spot them.)

Man 1: Man, I bet y'all been together for years. Y'all so cute together.

Romantic Dude: Nope. This is our first time meeting in person.

(He smiles at the woman, who smiles back, lovingly.)

Man 1: Well, she's a catch. A beauty. A catch.

Man 2: She's a piranha. King of the water. No. I'm sorry. Queen of the water. She's a piranha. She'll eat your ass alive.

Man 1: *(To woman)* Don't eat him, alright? Treat him good.

(The couple go back to romantically watching the French Quarter.)

(An older gentleman with an amazing, deep, melodious voice walks down the street, smiling and talking to no one in particular.)

Guy: I got gas! Y'all better keep your distance! I got gas! My stomach hurts, and I ain't sick! I got gas!

(He passes a girl, who smiles at him.)

Guy: Hey beautiful. *(Starts singing. Jazz style)* I got gas! I paid the gas bill! But I got gas!

(It is Thanksgiving night. The streets are empty, as most locals are at home with family, and few tourists come to New Orleans for Thanksgiving vacation. A middle-aged couple walk by the closed shops along Jackson Square, the woman holding a grocery bag, and the man holding a pizza with a bottle of liquor balanced on top.)

Woman: It's just a couple more blocks.

Man: Jesus! This is hard.

Woman: I can hold it for you. *(Pause)* The pizza! Not your penis.

(A man is standing in Jackson Square: the most touristy of the touristy spots in New Orleans. There are probably nearly a hundred people standing around taking selfies, looking at the displays set up by artists, listening to music, watching acrobats, and resting on the benches after a long day. The sun slowly sets, and a gentle breeze keeps the air from feeling too stagnant to breathe. A man, shirtless and verging on pantless, wanders back and forth in front of the Cathedral. He is weeping, hugging himself, and occasionally dropping to sit or roll on the flagstones. He is clearly having a very bad day.)

Guy: Someone hug me! Please! Give me a hug! I just need someone to hold me and tell me everything's going to be alright!

(A drunk girl stops, clearly feeling great empathy.)

Girl 1: OMG! Same!

(She starts to walk towards him with her arms open. Her friend grabs her arm.)

Girl 2: No, Shelia. *(To the guy)* We see you. We hear you. Everything will be alright, but no one's going to hold you until you pull up your pants.

(Daylight on Bourbon Street – bright enough that we can see how deep the grime is and how chunky the puddles are. A woman wearing a waitress' uniform stands half in/half out of the doorway to a bar. She is smoking and looks like this cigarette is giving her a glimpse of heaven. The dark bar is empty but for the bartender leaning on the walk-up service window. They are chatting with the deeply familiar tones of coworkers who see more of each other than they do their own families.)

Woman: I've never been fucked by a man, but I've fucked a Satan.

Bartender: *(Shaking his head)* This sure ain't Disneyland.

(A group walk down Bourbon Street towards the Clover Grill, one guy far behind the others.)

Girl: *(Turning back to yell at the straggler)* Ya helicoptering back there?

Guy: *(Shouting)* I ain't swinging no cocks!

(He runs a step or two to catch up, but slows back to walking a few yards behind the others.)

Guy: *(Mumbling under his breath)* I ain't swinging no cocks...

(A man dressed as gay Elvis – rainbow shirt, bell-bottoms, pompadour, sunglasses, and a good bit of sequins – walks down the street with some friends.)

Elvis: ... and she was like "Shake that Pelvis!" and I was like "Honey, I left my pelvis two blocks back."

(A guy walks down the street in his restaurant uniform with a thick coat over it. It is January, and it is the kind of wet, windy night that makes the cold feel so much colder than the temperature implies. The man is talking loudly on speakerphone. Whoever he is talking to is not loud enough to be heard as more than muffled electronic sounds.)

Guy: She's giving fellatio behind a bar.

(Pause)

Guy: *(More loudly)* I said, "She giving head behind a bar in the French Quarter!"

(Pause)

Guy: Well, I hope it can wait ten damn minutes. I just got off work. Can't you just wait till I get there?

(Pause)

Guy: Well, I took some insulin, and I'm on my way.

(Pause)

Guy: Well, damn, Vicki!

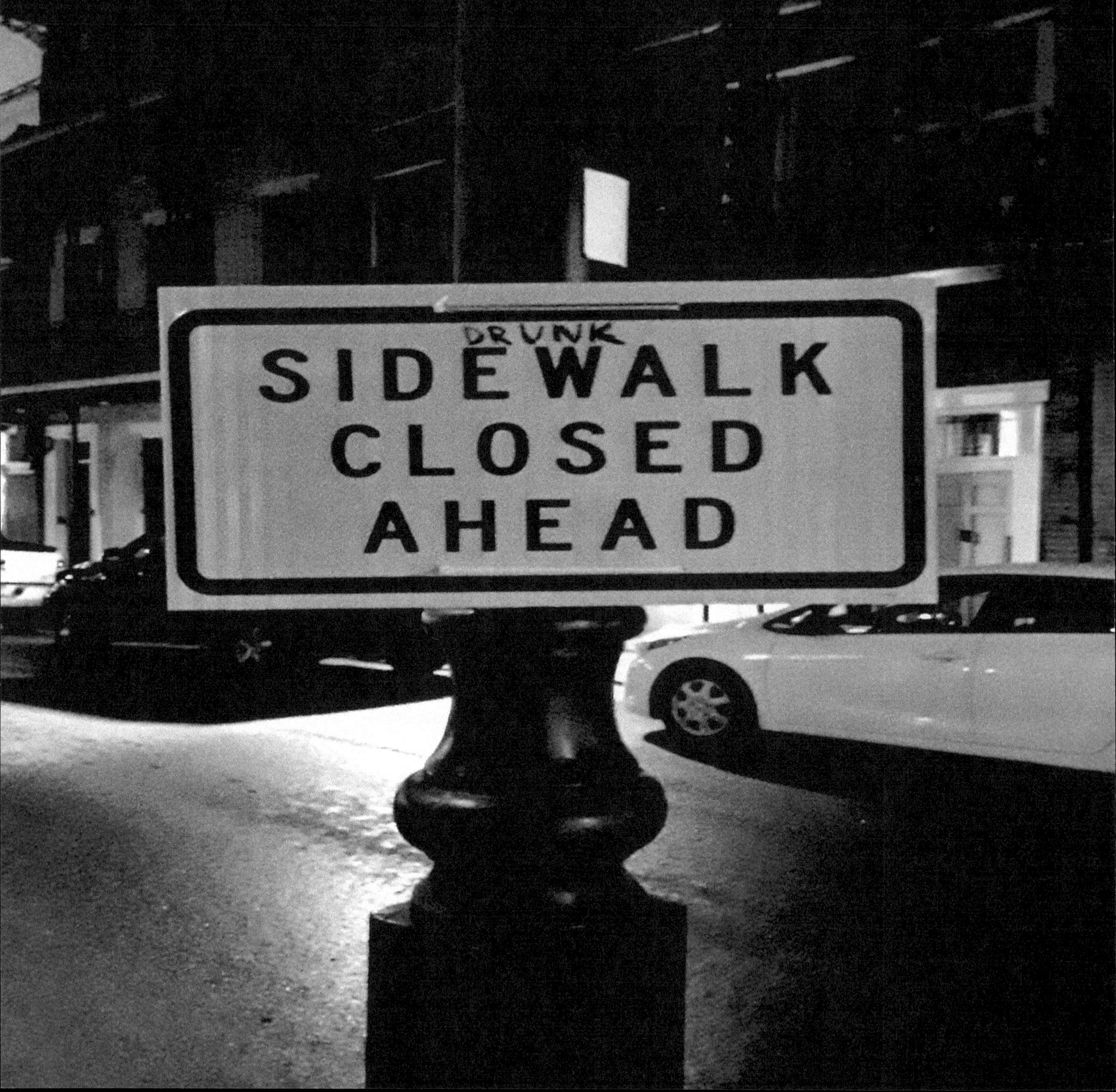
DRUNK
SIDEWALK
CLOSED
AHEAD

Where Y'at?

(A man rides a bicycle down Dauphine Street: a hurricane in one hand, the other bracing a pizza box up against the handlebars of his bike like a counterproductive windshield. He steers largely with his knees, swerving smoothly and elegantly around cars, potholes, and drunken tourists. A woman watches him.)

Woman: *(Laughing)* And that is proof God loves a fool.

(She trips over a spot of rough sidewalk.)

(A group stand around admiring the facade of a hotel on upper Chartres. Across the entrance, there is a lantern and light display, bright purple and blue lights making the place glow in the dark streets. One man is wearing a taco hat.)

Woman: The closer you get to the river, the higher you get.

Taco Hat: In Elevation?

Woman: That too.

(A group of four walk through Jackson Square, three carrying fishbowls, the fourth eating ice cream. Fishbowl 1 walks so far ahead it is not immediately apparent he is with the others. He stops to look back at his friends.)

Fishbowl 1: *(Shouting ten times louder than necessary)* Hey! Are you going to let me drive this boat?

Fishbowl 2: *(Also shouting)* Who you shouting at?!

Fishbowl 1: You! I'm asking you who's driving this boat!

Fishbowl 2: You asking me? Hell, no, you ain't driving. You're drunk!

Fishbowl 3: Then who's driving?

Fishbowl 2: I'm driving!

Fishbowl 1: Then drive! It looks to me like I'm driving this boat! And I'm drunk.

(Ice cream guy peacefully eats his ice cream. It looks like mint chocolate chip.)

(Two women stand on a corner surrounded by a press of drunks so thick you might as well be inside a club. Neon blinks around them, desperate to catch their attention. Beads hang from every surface horizontal enough to hold them. Five different bands blast covers of popular songs loud enough to rattle the teeth, and a Viking in full plastic armor with a Technicolor daiquiri in a plastic novelty cup chats with a cop. The smell is a heady mix of vomit, bleach, old beer, and pee. The two women look around in visible confusion.)

Women 1: No. This isn't Bourbon Street.

Women 2: Are you sure?

(It most definitely is Bourbon Street.)

(A party of four wander down the street, heading away from the busier sections of the Quarter. One woman walks ahead of the others, staring at her phone, very focused.)

Woman 1: *(Shouting at phone)* Where is it?!

Guy 1: I told you. Siri fucked up. She don't know shit! We should ask a human.

Guy 2: *(To the woman with the phone)* Ask her again.

Woman 1: *(Shouting at phone)* Where is it?!

Guy 1: Siri don't know.

Woman 1: *(Shouting at phone)* Where is it?!

Woman 2: Siri doesn't know what "it" is. Tell her where we are going.

Woman 1: No. She'll tell us where to go. *(To phone)* Where is it?!

(A tour walks by an older man who is sitting on the stairs leading up to a house. He is smoking a cigarette and is wearing a full-body, onesie-style lizard costume. He sees the tour, stands, drops his cigarette, and starts walking backwards in front of the group.)

Lizard: *(Gesturing at a building.)* Alright! To your right, you'll see a house, which is not for rent, because it's not haunted yet...

Tour Guest: Yet?

Lizard: That's right.

Tour Guest: Oh... uhm... Thank you?

Lizard: No. Thank you! And don't forget to tip your tour guide.

(He stops walking, so that the tour passes him by while he holds out his hand, ready to accept any tips. No one tips him.)

(Canal Street: the broad, brightly lit, highly commercial street that runs through the heart of New Orleans, separating the French Quarter from the Garden District. A group of middle-aged women, all wearing family reunion t-shirts personalized with their names, stop at an intersection, visibly lost.)

Woman 1: Is this the right way?

Woman 2: *(Shouting)* I think we should go down one of these little side alleys.

(She points down Royal Street, one of the main streets through the French Quarter. It is one block down from Bourbon and covered in antique shops and art galleries. It is not an alley.)

Woman 3: I don't know, Jemma. It looks dark. Is it safe? What's the address?

Woman 2: I want to go down that cute little alley!

Woman 1: NO, Jemma. We're trying to find the strip club!

(Three Pedicab drivers lounge around their cabs, sprawled across the back seats like beach chairs, waiting for guests. It is a foggy night. The air is heavy and damp. It is one of the odd nights where the Quarter is mostly very quiet, the silence only broken by roaming groups of drunken idiots shouting about how quiet it is.)

Pedicab 1: Man. It's fucking gorgeous tonight. The moon...

Pedicab 2: And it's been such a good night! Good tips. Nice tourists. I had this couple from Japan. They were so impressed by our moon.

Pedicab 1: Yeah man, I love tourists from Japan, because they don't have a moon there.

Pedicab 2: Really? Wild...

Pedicab 3: Man. What's with this rain?

(It is not raining.)

(A group of tourists turn a corner and start down Royal Street. They stop, turn around, and head the other direction before reversing a second time. They are clearly lost.)

Girl 1: Don't follow me! I'm dyslexic.

Girl 2: But how do you know?

Guy: *(With an authoritative tone)* She reads a lot of napkins.

(A group of college-aged kids walk by a building with a sign running down the bricks that reads "Hotel" right at eye level. Across the street, there is another hotel. Signs line the street saying "Hotel Parking." Through large bright windows we see a concierge sitting at a desk and a luggage cart by the door. One of the kids stops in front of the door, looking fascinated.)

Guy 1: Guys, wait! I think this might be a hotel!

Girl 1: Maybe it's a hostel?

Guy 1: No, look, it's a hotel! There's a brochure here by the door.

Girl 2: Oh My God! I didn't know there were hotels in the French Quarter! That's soooo cute!

Guy 2: Maybe we can stay down here next time we're in New Orleans.

Girl 1: I don't know... It's sort of far away from everything.

(They continue walking, turning onto Bourbon Street a block away.)

(A group of three tourists walk along the quiet end of Bourbon Street with someone we can assume to be a local.)

Local: Yeah, that was the Marigny.

Tourist: So, are we in the Quarter now?

Local: Yeah. Heading towards the CBD.

Tourist: And we're on Bourbon?

Local: Yeah.

Tourist: So, where is the Garden District?

Local: In the deepest core of the Ego.

(A troop of women with mussed hair in Fleur-de-Lis hoodies, with giant smiles and loud laughs, walk through a square. Oaks sway in the wind. The women cackle at each other.)

Woman 1: Man, she keeps getting her presidents wrong. Earlier today she called this Washington Square.

Woman 2: *(Laughing)* I know! I meant to say Benjamin Franklin!

Woman 1: Wrong president! Jefferson! Jefferson!

(They all laugh.)

(They are in Jackson Square.)

(The strip in front of Jackson Square along Decatur Street, where all the mule buggies park to wait for passengers. It is early in the night, but some people have clearly been drinking for hours. A couple stumble by, leaning into each other to stay upright, laughing warmly.)

Woman: I'm sorry. I didn't understand how this place works.

Guy: Oh my God! Look. It's a carousel!

(He points at the mules. The animals remain still and disinterested.)

(Jackson Square. Mardi Gras weekend. Most of the shops are closing up as we have reached the hour that the only people left out on the street are drunk or looking to get drunk. A collection of guys in Carhart jackets and camo baseball caps walk into a toy store, pushing by the worker trying to haul a giant toy soldier inside. They are each carrying a six pack of beer with at least one missing can.)

Store Clerk: Hey! You can't bring drinks in here.

Guy 1: Okay. But where can we get alcohol?

Guy 2: Yeah. Are drinks this way?

(He points down Decatur Street.)

Store Clerk: Drinks are all ways. There are bars in three directions.

Guy 1: Only three?

Store Clerk: The fourth is the river.

(They stumble away, towards the river.)

Silent Vignettes

(An electronic billboard flashes ads in front of the Superdome right at the point the raised highway turns towards the French Quarter. The ad shows a precious child in a school uniform smiling up at the text that reads, "Why Catholic School?"
(The ad changes.)
(An array of colorful daiquiris replaces the child's sweet face.)

(A man stands on the side of the road photographing a woman, who is photographing a guy on a Segway, who has paused to photograph a Bourbon Street sign.)

(On Royal Street, a band has set up a slack line between two iron gallery posts. A man in a faded button-up shirt and brown linen pants walks on the slack line like he is at the circus, while playing a cheerful jig on the violin. He is accompanied by a girl in a light cotton sundress and no shoes, playing an accordion. Their dog watches from the curb, his chin resting on his dirty paws.)

(Royal Street. One block from Bourbon Street. A nine-foot-tall demon stands on the banquette. Under the black, pleather costume, he is a street performer on stilts. Neon spikes and frills poke out along his form, giving him something of a playful, raver look. He wears a mask with a broad grin, multi-colored neon teeth, and red lights in his eyes. The mask is pushed up to reveal the face of the man beneath, who is currently leaning down to speak to a police officer. The officer has out a small notebook where he is recording details. Our demon is reporting a fight he saw further down Royal Street.)

(A large group of college students, all wearing matching t-shirts proclaiming them to be members of a Christian university, stand in the center of an intersection. Our Christian choir take their time, forming up into lines and posing for a photo in front of a house where, two hundred years ago, an unknown number of people were horrifically tortured. Cars are backed up at least a block in both directions, honking loudly. The photographer turns as one car inches up, clearly hoping to squeeze past the group or possibly hoping to remind the group that these are not pedestrian-only streets. The photographer smiles and waves at the driver before turning back to the group to take another photo. The honking gets louder.)

(On the highway just beyond the French Quarter there is a sobriety checkpoint. It is visible from the top of an overpass, and as we approach, slowing, we spot some detritus on the side of the road. A large daiquiri cup spins on the asphalt, a stream of still partially frozen beverage trailing from where the wind took it when it was thrown from a moving vehicle.)

(A party bus rolls by going the other direction with music throbbing, strobe lights flashing, and fog drifting from the window.)

(Bourbon Street. The quiet end. The bars are three blocks behind us. All that is ahead is a residential neighborhood, and if the tourists don't get lost along the way, Frenchman Street. A group of women walk down the center of the street, drinking, chatting, laughing, and having a good time. A car comes up behind them, stopping because they are blocking the street.)

(They do not move.)

(The car flashes their headlights to declare their presence.)

(The girls do not step aside.)

(Finally, the car honks. One girl waves. The others drop it like it's hot and start twerking on the car hood.)

(There is no music except for the now-insistent honking.)

(We are in front of a bar on Burgundy Street. This is the area out beyond Bourbon Street, where speed limits become an illusion and stop signs just decoration. A woman is trying to back her car across an intersection to reach a parking spot she spotted too late. Cars behind her creep up, hoping to slip around her. From the other direction cars roll through the intersection, stopping for neither her, nor the stop sign. A man in tight shorts watches for a moment, waves at the woman, and steps out into traffic with his hand held out like a crossing guard to stop the cars. He twerks to entertain the drivers while they wait. The woman gives him a high-five out the window as she backs past him. No one honks.)

(Bourbon Street. A Friday night. The streets are full of people wandering from bar to bar and people-watching with neon-colored drinks in cheap plastic cups in their hands. There is a group of four adolescent boys drumming on old pickle tubs for tips on the corner. A woman stops to dance. She has clearly forgotten she is wearing a tube top. It rolls down, exposing her to the group of barely teenaged pickle tub drummers. She drops her drink as she reaches desperately to pull her top back up. The boys are nonplussed.)

Rude, Nasty, and Sticky Streets

(A mom and son, probably around 12, walk down the street. As he walks, the boy reaches out to touch a hitching post, a lamp post, a stop sign, a fence, a shutter, etc. He touches everything in arm's reach along his way.)

Mother: I've told you, stop touching things! You're not allowed to touch anything in New Orleans. STOP!

(The boy looks at her, then reaches out to touch a fire hydrant.)

(It is an aggressively warm summer night. A woman is sitting on the stoop of what is presumably her house, wearing pajama shorts and slippers. She is talking on the phone and smoking a cigarette.)

Woman: I don't think it's roaches, because someone saw a opossum in the laundry room...

(There is a pause while whoever she is talking to responds. She takes a long drag on the cigarette.)

Woman: No. I don't think it's tear gas.

(A woman stands on a dark sidewalk, typing on her phone. The streets are mostly quiet, though less than a block away, music booms out of a dark-windowed bar. A man stumbles up the street. He stops in front of an iron gate that guards an alley leading back to one of the courtyards which loom behind most houses in the Quarter. The man turns towards the gate, then stops, and looks at the woman.)

Man: Do you live here?

Woman: Like in the city? Yeah.

Man: No. Like here. *(Waves at the gate)*

Woman: At this house? No.

Man: Cool.

(He turns back towards the gate, unzips, and starts to pee. The woman glances over, and seeing penis, quickly walks away.)

(It is Easter. The French Quarter is relatively quiet, with a few revelers left over from the earlier parades still rambling the streets. A tour guide stands by a little park, under the looming shadows of oaks and oleanders. She extols the deeds of murderers from the 1800s to a crowd of tipsy tourists. An older lady in a bright purple shirt and broad brimmed red hat walks by. She reaches out and slaps the guide's ass.)

Old Lady: *(Shouting)* Tell 'em about the Vampires!

(Two guys stop to take a picture of the drug store where they still rent out movies. Behind them, two girls walk by having a very loud conversation with very large daiquiris in hand.)

Girl 1: You know my urine is fine.

Girl 2: Yeah, I know. I'm jealous.

Guy: *(Turning to the girls)* Yeah, me too!

(Two men walk down Royal Street. One is wearing a tank top and shorts in forty-degree weather. The other is wearing a poofy jacket like you would wear to go skiing. They pass the Cornstalk Fence Hotel, in front of which there is a cast iron fence that was designed to look like a row of corn stalks growing towards the sky. To enhance the "realism" the ears of corn have been painted bright yellow. It is still unmistakably a fence, not actual plants.)

Shorts: Eek! *(This is not him screaming. This is the word, "Eek")* It's Corn! I LOOVE Corn!

(He grabs the fence, trying to shake it.)

Shorts: I want to Eat it! Eek! Let's eat corn!

(He kneels before the fence, gnawing on the metal.)

Jacket: *(Mumbling)* Yes... I totally love corn...

(Jacket grabs the fence, pulling himself up to it, and begins humping the metal.)

(A woman rides by in a pedicab, the wheels bumping along the pot-hole strewn asphalt as jazzy music sings out from a portable speaker clipped to the driver's belt. The driver's face is red and covered in sweat, but he still manages to maintain a conversation with his patron.)

Woman: I heard about this girl who got abducted off of Bourbon Street and ended up somewhere crazy....

Pedicab Driver: Yeah, I don't think we do abductions here.

(It is a busy night in the Quarter. There are about seven million tours lined up in front of the more famous locations. Ghost tours, vampire tours, witch tours, voodoo tours, true crime tours, history tours, pub crawls, and even a pirate tour or two vie for prime locations close enough for a good view of whichever building they are talking about but far enough away from each other to maintain the sense of creepiness. A group of men carrying Huge Ass Beers walk behind a row of tour guests.)

(Guy 1 makes a funny face.)

Guy 2: Did you try it?

Guy 1: Yeah man. I tried my best.

Guy 3: To do what?

Guy 1: To drop a cloud on them.

Guy 3: What?

Guy 1: I've been trying all night to fart on one of those tours. Leave them in a cloud of stank.

(Guy 1 and Guy 2 share a high-five.)

(A group of three stand on a street corner. We can see Touchdown Jesus down one street – the shadow's wide embracing arms like a perpetual celebration – and skyscrapers rising into the clouds down the other. The man in the group wears a Hawaiian shirt and a tour guide badge. The two women wear socks with sandals and fanny packs. The man gestures towards the streets, which glisten in the strange combination of neon and gas lighting that marks the French Quarter.)

Tour Guide: Yeah. New Orleans is a magical wonderland! Penis-glitter everywhere!

(A man walks down the quiet end of Bourbon, towards the chaos, leading a group that one might assume are his family. They all have a similar look to them and all look overheated in the only mildly hot weather. He looks down at something on the sidewalk.)

Man: This is the city of disgustings.

(He belches, loudly.)

(Two women walk by the front of Jackson Square where all the buggies are parked. One of the girls runs over to pet a mule. Being slightly inebriated, she misses, and pokes it in the face. It nibbles on her hand.)

Girl 1: Ewwwwwwwwww. It bit me.

(Tries to pet it again)

Girl 2: Oh my god! It did it again.

(Another girl is walking by, but stops, looking irritated.)

Girl 3: Maybe stop poking it in the face. Did you even ask if you could pet him?

Girl 1: Mind your own business.

(She again reaches to pet this most patient of all mules.)

Girl 3: Oh my god! Just stop. Leave the poor animal alone.

Girl 2: You leave us alone!

(As we continue past, the argument escalates. By the time we reach the corner, the three girls are screaming at the top of their lungs.)

Girl 1: You're a Nosy Fucking Bitch!

(Pirates Alley. The comparatively narrow path between St. Louis Cathedral and the Cabildo. These are two of the most recognizable historic buildings in the city. The alley lets out into Jackson Square, the heart of tourist territory. There are families with small children and lost suburbanites everywhere. There are four walking tours within visible distance. The bar halfway down the alley is overflowing with cheerful patrons. A man is walking down the alley quickly, with his head down. Behind him marches a lady screaming at him.)

Man: Leave me alone!

Woman: I would if you weren't peeing in public. Near elementary school kids. Against a church.

Man: I had to go.

Woman: And you decided our church was your toilet?

Man: Just leave me alone.

Woman: Maybe you won't do it again if you learn some shame. Hey! EVERYONE! This guy's a church pisser! He peed on our church! Church Pisser! Church Pisser! Shame the Church Pisser!

(They head around the corner, the woman still shouting. An exceptionally loud taunt carries from offstage.)

Woman: HE'S A LEAKY CAULDRON!

(Jackson Square. Around twenty people – some casually sipping drinks, some looking excited, some already looking unfocused – stand in a half-circle around a tour guide. The guide is just starting her introduction, explaining the rules to the group. People walking by look over at them curiously. Most decide this clearly has nothing to do with them. One very intoxicated woman pushes through the group to stand directly in front of the guide.)

Woman: So, when were these trees put in?!

Tour Guide: What?

Woman: Like how old are these trees?

Tour Guest: Tell her to pay you. She ain't on our tour!

(A group of middle-aged, middle-class people walk along Royal Street wearing enough beads, flowers, glittery hats, and general parade bling to supply a party store.)

Guy: It's just a couple of blocks down here.

Woman: *(With a sharp Midwestern accent)* Along the way, are there any dark alleys where we can stop and buy some stolen porn?

(We are in front of St. Louis Cathedral, right by the statue of Pope John Paul II. A middle-aged couple walk by quietly arguing.)

Woman: No. You can get that. New Orleans is a collection of drug dealer perverts.

(Five dude-bros walk down a relatively quiet section of Royal Street. They pass a tour, quietly listening to a guide tell a historical tale of violence and death. The guide is melodramatically drawing out the events, painting in sharp details, and explaining historical context. This is clearly the climax of the story. All the guests are leaning in, with various looks of horror, curiosity, and excitement on their face. The bros pause behind the tour.)

Bro 1: *(Roaring)* WIKIPEDIA!!!!

Bro 2: Dude, why are you such an instigator?

(They high-five. Across the street, a car alarm starts blaring.)

Tour Guest: Instigator? More like asshole.

(A group of hipsters stand in front of an art gallery. There's a party happening inside that has spilled out onto the street. A banjo player and an accordionist perform surrounded by paintings of what look like glamour shots from the eighties with the phrase "Fuck the Eighties" plastered across the canvases.)

Hipster 1: Do you want some?

Hipster 2: Maybe human bone tastes like marshmallow...

(Thanksgiving night in the Quarter. It is quiet. Presumably most people are home with their families. A group of men congregate around a bar, having a beer and enjoying the camaraderie. A group of college-age bros wander down the street.)

Bro 1: *(Reading each address off the buildings)* 1020! 1022! Dude!

Bro 2: *(Looking at his phone)* Yeah. But where's the Quarter?

Bro 1: 1024!

Bro 2: We've got to find the Quarter. Stop shouting numbers. You're confusing Google Maps.

Bro 3: Dude, do you see a trash can?

(There is a trash can right in front of him.)

Bro 2: We're in New Orleans. Throw it anywhere. The entire city is a trash can!

(He takes his friend's beer bottle and throws it into the street. Several of the men at the bar turn to glare at him.)

Man: Could you not?! Drunk tourists are NOT what I'm thankful for!

64

Wisdom

(A family is on a tour, walking swiftly past Bourbon Street. The mother has her hand on the ten-year-old boy's shoulder, steering him past the chaos.)

Boy: *(Looking back)* But isn't there anything to see on Bourbon Street?

Mother: No.

Father: Not really.

Tour Guide: Nope.

(They move on quickly while a woman dressed like a stripper version of a cop uses a riding crop to spank a bachelorette wearing beads with plastic penises dangling like charms on a charm bracelet.)

(Half a block from Bourbon Street, a man sits on the nasty sidewalk amongst chunky puddles and black patches that are hopefully just dirt built up on old gum. He is talking to two guys standing over him. All three have scraggly beards and cigarette burns on their fingers. They look like they might have been rolling around on Bourbon Street all night.)

Man: You know, your shoe can fall off when you're dead.

(All three laugh.)

(It is a quiet Sunday afternoon. People dressed in church clothes leave St. Louis Cathedral, tourists watching them curiously. Two men sit on the benches in front of the church. One is wearing a New Orleans Saints' jersey and has the look of someone who probably slept in their clothes. The other is draped in enough Mardi Gras beads that they could be nothing but a tourist. They both have Huge Ass Beers.)

Jersey Guy: And then I prayed, and Jesus took care of me! Basically, I'm the reason the Saints won the Superbowl...

Beads Guy: *(Heavily slurring)* Someone should write an article on that!

Jersey Guy: They really should.

Beads Guy: I'd read that!

Jersey Guy: I wouldn't.

(Two men walk down the more residential part of Ursulines Street. This is an area that has nothing but homes with maybe a store on the corner. Guy 1 walks into a tree. Its trunk is only about as broad as a man's thigh, but it has been there long enough for the roots to push up the sidewalk like a little mountain range all around it. He bounces off the trunk and stumbles into the house next to him.)

Guy 1: Dude, what's a tree doing in the city!?

Guy 2: Well, you know.... Hurricanes.

(A man lays in the gutter of Toulouse Street, right off of Bourbon. He smiles as wide as the Mississippi River. He shows no desire to get up. A group of tourists pass, glancing at him nervously.)
Guy: Sometimes you fall. When you're having a one-man parade. Man, sometimes you fall.

(A trio of beautifully dressed, beautifully made-up young women clack by in surprisingly high heels. One of them is finishing a story.)
Girl 1: ... and I did! But I still needed to get to work, so I...
Girl 2: You know, it's not okay to stab people, like ever.
Girl 1: *(Sighs)* I KNOW...

(A group of gutter-punks hang around in front of a closed souvenir shop, some sitting, some lounging on their backpacks. They are smoking what is probably not a cigarette.)

Younger Man: What? Do you think you're immortal?

Older Man: Course not. I feel like I could be killed by bullets, but I'd prefer books.

Younger Man: *(Miming a tipping bookcase)* Like falling?

Older Man: Naw. Just killed by books.

(Four well-dressed African-American women walk down the street. They look like they are coming from a conference, with sharp, tailored slacks, brightly patterned blouses, and badges hanging from lanyards. One is carrying a stack of books, another a notebook with a pile of loose papers sticking out from between the pages.)

Woman 1: I keep telling myself, "You have got to learn to write with the confidence of a mediocre white woman!"

(Two men sit on the stoop before a store: one old, one young. Both look like they've seen better days. One holds a sign asking for donations to buy them booze. A tourist walks by and mutters something unintelligible but clearly rude.)

Older Man: Man, there are a lot of shitty people out tonight. But you can't let them make you into a shitty person, or you're just as bad.

(The young man nods, sagely.)

(It is a foggy night, the air just muggy enough that everything feels sticky. The sound of distant trumpet drips out of the fog, the moisture in the air making it impossible to place where it is coming from. Two gutter-punks walk peacefully down the street, past a woman who is sitting on a car, obviously waiting for something.)

Gutter-punk 1: It's fine. No matter what, Bourbon Street will still be there.

Gutter-punk 2: Yeah, like, the city will burn, and from the ashes Bourbon Street will rise.

Woman: It will float. When the city sinks, Bourbon will still be there with drunks stumbling off the sidewalks and drowning in the street.

Gutter-punks 1: Naw, it's like in a car crash where only the drunk walks away safe, cause they went limp. The drunks will float down the middle of the street like litter in the canal, while the sludge of the city rises around them.

(Two guys sprawl on the steps around Jackson Square in dirty old band shirts.)
Guy 1: This girl kept trying to tell me life is good. *(He laughs)* I mean...
Guy 2: *(Taking a heavy drag off his cigarette)* Yeah. Life is life.

(A clearly intoxicated man sits on the steps in front of the locked gate of Jackson Square. He is alone. Tourists walk by without giving him a second glance. A group of gutter-punks stand near the church listening to a story one of their number is telling about a roommate who never cleans up after herself. A group of twenty-something girls get a tarot card reading, interrupting the reader to pick on each other and laugh gleefully. It is pleasant except for our drunk friend.)
Drunk Guy: *(Shouting)* You better work harder, because Spider-Man ain't coming to save you.
(The gutter-punks pause, look at him, and go back to their story. The tourists look away. No one responds.)
Drunk Guy: Not Robin either.
(No one responds.)
Drunk Guy: *(Muttering quietly to himself)* Definitely not Robin. Fucker.

(Jackson Square. It has been misting and raining all day. The water turns the flagstones into a mirror, reflecting back the streetlights and the shadows. Only a few tourists linger in the atmospheric, but damp, public space. A woman walks out of the fog between the Cathedral and the Cabildo. She is shouting into the ether.)

Woman: That's a foul! A foul like the Saints should have got. Where's the patrol? I need a patrol.

(She spots a tour guide leaning against a lamp post.)

Woman: Are you the patrol? Will you patrol me?

Tour Guide: No. I'm a tour guide.

Woman: *(Continuing on her way)* I need someone to patrol me. I need someone.

(Several dude-bros wander away from Bourbon Street, talking loudly. They have the gait of people who have been drinking several hours too long.)

Guy 1: Yeah, man. Life is terrible, and then you come to New Orleans, and everything is better.

Guy 2: And drunker.

Guy 1: Yeah, man. *(Pause)* I should just become a vampire.

(A couple stand on the side of the road in front of a historical home. They are fighting under the watchful eye of a half-dozen gutter-punks and some rather lost looking tourists.)

Woman: Then I'm calling you 'a male'.

Man: *(Holding his hands up defensively)* I don't know, now. Don't get me wrong.

Woman: Oh hell no. You're not going to stand there and call me "a female" while you call a man "a man." You ain't disrespecting me like that. Either it's "female and male" or "a man and a woman."

Gutter-punk: Hell yeah!

(A woman stands in front of St. Louis Cathedral, talking ninety-to-nothing towards two much calmer companions. She looks like she has spent half her life on a fishing boat: skin tanned to a rich leather brown, surprisingly muscular arms, wearing a baseball cap with several lures hooked into it. Her companions look like they walked out of a different side of America: both in crisp button-up shirts, the man with nicely pressed slacks and his partner in a calf-length skirt and kitten heels.)

Woman: Well, you know Jesus hung out with thieves and drunks. So, I'm just like, "What would Jesus do?"

Guy: Not Bourbon Street, I'm guessing.

Woman: Yeah. I guess you're right. He'd probably tell me to go to sleep it off. Which, sure. Fuck, yeah!

Guy: *(Clearly deeply offended)* Excuse me!

Woman: Oh yeah. *(To statue of the Pope next to her)* Sorry, Jeezy.

Glossary

Banquette: What sidewalks are officially called in New Orleans. A great term to show off that you know more about New Orleans than most tourists.

Cabildo: One of the three big buildings that sit along the back of Jackson Square. It was a government building during the colonial years. Now, it's a museum.

CBD: The Central Business District. If you are in the French Quarter and see buildings over four stories, you are looking at the CBD. Alternately, it's something that you can buy from a lot of places that have green leaves all over their signs.

Daiquiri: A very sweet, very frozen, very alcoholic drink that costs too much and may or may not come in a cheap plastic souvenir cup.

Fishbowl: A very sweet, very alcoholic drink that is bright blue and comes in a cheap plastic souvenir fishbowl.

Fleur de Lis: A heraldic lily. Also, a traditional symbol of New Orleans. You'll see it on cast iron fences, t-shirts, hats, bumper stickers, signs, flags, Mardi Gras beads, and separating scenes in this book.

Garden District: The area with all those beautiful old mansions that you see in movies about New Orleans or that you read about in Anne Rice books.

Gallery: What most places call a balcony. But only the ones that go all the way across the banquette and have supports that go to the ground. Balconies are the ones that only have supports that angle off the buildings to which they are attached. *
*Only tour guides and people whose entire identity revolves around living in New Orleans care about the difference between balconies and galleries.

Gutter-punks: The young folks you'll see along Decatur Street and Frenchmen Street wearing ratty band shirts, patched and dirty denim, and a fine patina of French Quarter grime. They smoke, they have funny signs, they will be nice to you if you are nice to them, and because a lot of them crash in interesting places, they don't always smell great. They don't always like the term "gutter-punk."

Huge Ass Beer: Predictably, this is a very large beer. The same bar also serves Half-Ass Beers, if the Huge Ass Beer is too much for you. They come in plastic souvenir cups.

Hand Grenade: A very sweet, very frozen, very alcoholic drink that costs too much and comes in a cheap plastic souvenir cup that is shaped like a hand grenade.

Hurricane: Either a storm you should probably leave town for, or a drink that is very sweet, very alcoholic, and red enough that locals can guess what you've been drinking from your vomit.

Krewe: A social organization. Parade Krewes build floats, learn dances, and make costumes for parades. Bike Krewes form large groups and ride around the city having fun. Many krewes do charitable works and organize community events.

Marigny: The neighborhood next to the French Quarter where the cool young people live. It's pronounced "Mare In E," but for a fun time, have your GPS try to say it.

Pedicabs: A bicycle taxi. They operate primarily in the French Quarter. The drivers tell sometimes accurate, often ridiculous stories, and have amazing legs. Don't forget to tip.

Pirate's Alley: The alley that runs between St. Louis Cathedral and the Cabildo. It may be the most French Quarter spot you will ever see. There's a bar, a bookstore, a mask shop, a lingerie shop, ghost stories, the Cathedral, and usually the faint lingering smell of urine.

Southern Decadence: A party/street festival that happens Labor Day weekend in the French Quarter. It's flamboyant, adult, kinky, LGBTQIA, and decadent. Some people refer to it as the less corporate version of Pride.

Touchdown Jesus: The statue of Jesus in Pere Antoine's Garden, behind St. Louis Cathedral. He holds his arms out to embrace the world, unless you walk down past Bourbon and look back. Then his shadow looks like he's holding his arms up to signal someone scored in football.

Where Y'at: A phrase so common in New Orleans it has come to define a dialect native to the city. It literally means "Where are you?" but it is more often used to ask "How are you?" or "What's up?" or "What are you up to?"

Elaine Allen was raised in Mississippi, but spent her childhood visiting New Orleans, where she took great pride in the fact that tourists would often ask her for directions. She attended the Mississippi School of the Arts and Bennington College, where she studied theatre and literature. After college she spent years in New Hampshire teaching theatre classes for elementary, middle, and high school students. Walking to work one day through over a foot of ice-coated snow, she suddenly wondered why she wasn't in New Orleans. As a mature and responsible adult, she picked up her life and drove back down south. She has worked as a ghost tour guide for almost a decade, sharing the history and legends of the French Quarter with thousands of tourists. She now lives happily with her four cats – all named after historic New Orleans figures – writing, and trying to survive the endless New Orleans heat.

You can find her on YouTube discussing books, writing, and sharing ridiculous stories of things that happen on her tours.

Printed in the USA
CPSIA information can be obtained
at www.ICGtesting.com
LVHW081315261023
762209LV00071B/1759